Worry

"God, why am I worried?"

By Lisa Keyne

Edited by Jane L. Fryar

Editorial assistant: Marilyn T. Weber

This publication is also available in braille and in large print for the visually impaired. Write to the Library for the Blind, 1333 South Kirkwood Road, St. Louis, MO 63122-7295. Allow six months for processing.

3558 South Jefferson Avenue, St. Louis, MO 63118-3968
Manufactured in the United States of America.

1 2 3 4 5 6 7 8 9 10 03 02 01 00 99 98 97 96 95 94

By mutual agreement . . .
and in the Holy Spirit's power

We will rely on the Holy Scriptures as our final authority,
knowing that human ideas and opinions,
even the ideas and opinions of God's people, will
likely stray from God's truth from time to time.

We will listen to each other and show one another
Christ-like love and concern.

We will contribute to the discussion in positive ways
as we are able to do that.

We will use what we learn in this group to contribute
even more fully to the overall ministry of

____

(*Put your congregation's name here.*)

We will attend each session unless an
emergency prevents our attendance.

We will respect one another's schedules by
beginning and ending on time.

We will keep everything we hear in this group confidential,
sharing it with no one unless doing so
is a matter (literally) of life and death.

Contents

How to Use This Course

Three ingredients will make it possible for you to maximize the usefulness of this course.

❖ 1—Spirit-Led Prayer

Only as God invades our lives and touches our hearts can we grow up in Him. Ask and keep on asking for the Holy Spirit's direction and help as you approach His Word. Even if you work through the questions in this study on your own (and perhaps especially then), you must rely on God to do His work in you, His holy work of drawing you to Himself. He's the only one who can connect us to Himself and keep that connection strong. He's the only one who can connect us to our brothers and sisters in the faith and keep those connections strong. We need to ask Him to do that.

❖ 2—Spirit-Led Care

That is, care for one another in your group. Dietrich Bonhoeffer once wrote, "Christianity means community through Jesus Christ and in Jesus Christ . . . we belong to one another only through and in Jesus Christ."

Only God can create the kind of care, the kind of community, the kind of connectedness that we see modeled by the early Christian church. It's His gift to His people, wrought by the power of the Holy Spirit working through Word and Sacrament. We can't make it happen, no matter how slick our techniques, no matter how smooth our approach.

God does this as we live in His grace through the forgiveness of sins received in Word and Sacrament. It is this Word and Sacrament that provides the kind of faith, the kind of acceptance in which His people come to know one another as brothers and sisters in the faith, and not as third or fourth cousins. Living by faith we, as the children of God, mirror the image of our Father, as did Jesus.

❖ 3—Spirit-Led As We Share

How does that kind of love happen? We cannot drum it up by our own effort, no matter how up-to-date our methodology. Rather, God will gift us with caring hearts through His Word and Sacraments. Neither can we force any believer or group of believers to talk about their faith with one another, to share their needs and hurts with each other, or to admonish and console one another. We can, however, use what we know about human relationships to create a safe haven, an island of time and place, in which God's people can relax, get to know one another, and, eventually, feel free to be honest and open in sharing of joys and doubts and concerns in their life with God.

In this kind of setting, participants can experience the freedom to talk about their hurts and their faith with each other, if they choose to do that. They can encourage one another in the one true faith, just as the early Christians did and as the holy apostles also urge us to do as God's chosen people today (1 Thessalonians 4:18; 5:11).

❖ On to the Practical

As you develop small-group ministry in your congregation, you need to keep an overarching vision in mind. But to get small-group Bible study off the ground, and to keep it functioning effectively, you also need to think through some practical considerations.

Leadership

Talk with your pastor about this. He has both the right and the duty to oversee any Bible-study program in your congregation. He himself may lead some groups. And he may decide to delegate some leadership tasks, approving those who will teach and taking care to see that they receive adequate training.

In general, all those who lead small-group Bible studies will be people who

- demonstrate an understanding of Law and Gospel, sin and grace, not just intellectually, but in their relationships with God and with other people ;
- demonstrate an ability to communicate the truths of the Scriptures clearly;
- express a desire to be used by God to disciple others;
- know or be willing to learn techniques that enable adults to examine and apply their faith to their daily lives;
- pray for the group and the congregation regularly;
- have time to plan, prepare, and lead a small-group Bible study on an ongoing, consistent basis;
- demonstrate the emotional and spiritual maturity to accept responsibilities of leadership, to receive direction and sometimes criticism with wisdom and grace, to share personal strengths and weaknesses with appropriate vulnerability, and to respond to others with Christ-like humility and love.

Setting

Many people find a home conducive to the relaxed, casual atmosphere you want to foster. In any case, you will need a meeting place where

- from 6–10 people can sit comfortably and see one another as they converse;
- the chairs are comfortable;
- the room is suitably lighted, ventilated, and at a comfortable temperature;
- coffee, tea, or soft drinks and an occasional snack can be served without danger of damaging carpets or upholstery;
- children can be adequately supervised while they play away from the Bible-study group.

Supplies

Everyone who attends should bring his or her own Bible. In addition you will need

- copies of this Study Guide for everyone (note the leaders materials in the back of this guide);
- pens or pencils, one for everyone;

- songbooks, hymnals, and perhaps an instrument to accompany singing during worship times;
- an empty chair or two placed prominently to remind everyone of the opportunity to invite guests—in particular, unchurched friends or relatives.

❖ That First Meeting

The first time you're together, you will want to spend some time getting to know one another and establishing rules for the group.

- Introduce yourselves to one another. Do this even if only one person is unfamiliar to the others. Tell your name. Tell a little about your family. And tell how you've come to be in the group. Use a timer and allow each person to speak for about one minute.
- Agree on ground rules about questions like these:

  Who will bring snacks? How often?

  Will we provide childcare? If so, how? Will we take turns, hire someone and agree to all chip in to pay for it? Or?

  Will we meet in one location? Take turns hosting the group? Or?

  When will we begin? End? (Include dates and also times.)
- Read the "By Mutual Agreement" statement located on page 3 of this guide. Talk it over until everyone understands it and you truly have reached mutual agreement. Promise to reread this agreement as you begin each session, at least the first several times you get together.
- Talk about participation. This study asks group members to work with partners or with three or four other people. Agree to listen to one another with respect. Also agree to allow one another the freedom to "pass" on any question for any reason without having to state that reason.
- Remind one another that everyone is entitled to an opinion. However, in this group all human opinions must take a back seat to the Holy Scriptures. You will share lots of thoughts and feelings with one another during the next few weeks. At least you will, if this course is written well, and

your leader(s) encourage participation as they should. Even so, we believe that absolute truth exists and that it can be known because the God who created the universe has revealed the truth for us in His Word. We bow to His wisdom. We submit to His truth.

❖ Elements of Small-Group Bible Studies

Most groups spend 60–90 minutes together in these four activities:

- Worship
- Bible study
- Prayer
- Fellowship

Worship (5–15 minutes)

As most small-group Bible studies begin, participants spend a few minutes in worship. Often this includes singing, especially if someone in the group can play the guitar or piano. If the group does not include a musician, someone in the group can usually find an alternative that will allow everyone to join in singing two or three hymns or songs. Some groups find that they manage to sing quite well a cappella. Some use prerecorded accompaniment tracks from cassette tapes or CDs.

Keep in mind, though, that worship involves much more than simply singing a few random songs. Worship should help participants quiet their hearts as the Lord prepares them to hear what He will say to them in His Word.

Therefore, opening worship will almost always include a prayer for His peace and for hearts ready to receive His truth.

Bible Study (40–60 minutes)

Our relationship with our Lord deepens as we immerse ourselves in His Word. In that Word He confronts us with our sin and then comforts us with His forgiving love in our Savior. Small-group Bible study at its best provides for both those processes to take place.

Materials appropriate for small-group study avoid a lecture format. Rather, they involve a mix of individual thought and writing, one-on-one discussions, and give-and-take conversations by the whole group. The leader facilitates, asks questions, provides nuggets of insight to push the group's process forward, and prays for participants while they think and talk with one another.

Prayer—(5–10 minutes)

In the small-group Bible-study process, God's Word touches the hearts of His people. It probes pockets of hurt and sometimes of hardness. God's people talk with one another about life's most important issues. We think and laugh together. We question and cry together. It's only natural that we pray together too. It's not only natural, but necessary.

This kind of prayer models itself after that of the early church:

> They raised their voices together in prayer to God. . . . After they prayed, the place where they were meeting was shaken. And they were all filled with the Holy Spirit and spoke the word of God boldly. (Acts 4:24, 31)

Committed by God's grace to one another and to the truth of His Word, God's people asked their Lord to intervene in their lives. Together they asked for His specific help with specific challenges and needs. They united their hearts in praise to Him for all He had done and for all that He had promised yet to do. They received from Him the power they needed to live as His witnesses in a world that is, even now for the most part, hostile to the claims of Christ. We join them in the same kind of prayer.

Fellowship (10–20 minutes)

Christian fellowship means so much more than this

spring's softball league or last Friday's fish fry. Of course, there is nothing wrong with playing softball or sharing a meal with other believers. But God intends that Christian fellowship (*koinonia*) cut more deeply below life's surface than that.

As we said earlier, only God can create genuine fellowship. It's His gift to His people. We can, however, provide unstructured time over coffee or lemonade before and after the more formal group time. This will free participants to laugh together, to cry together, to ask one another about ongoing personal and family concerns and simply to enjoy one another as members of God's family.

We witness spontaneously to one another about what God has done for us in Christ's cross and, then too, about what He is doing for us in our day-to-day lives. We have the chance to share specific prayer requests one-on-one and to become aware of needs God would use us to meet for each other. In short, we have a chance to be the church, the family of God, for one another.

❖ How to Use This Course

Remember Alfred E. Newman and his motto? Who, me, worry? Many of us grinned and admired his chutzpah during our days in elementary school or junior high.

But then we grew up. We became the ones paying the bills. We took on the responsibility of house or car, babies or aging parents. We took over the profit and loss statement for the farm, factory, or family business.

Who, me, worry? Yes. Me. And quite a lot at times. Despite my Lord's promises. Despite His faithful love demonstrated again and again. Even despite His commitment to me as He bled and died on Calvary's cross. Yes. Me. I do worry. I don't want to worry. But I do. And I don't know quite what to do about it.

This course addresses worry head-on. It confronts both the "little worries" and the fire-breathing dragons of worry that singe our necks when the sky falls in on us.

Session 1 defines worry and helps participants identify specific areas of worry that most often trip us up. It goes on to delineate God's process for overcoming worry—the process of repentance.

Session 2 zeros in on God's powerful promises to defend us even if the earth itself moves off its axis. It leads participants to consider how the desire to control our own lives can lead us into worry and through worry into deep fear. It takes participants through the difficult process of relinquishing control and putting their lives back into the Savior's strong and loving hands.

Session 3 looks at worrisome situations at the outer limits of personal threat—unemployment, bankruptcy, natural disasters, and death itself. It suggests ways that Christ's suffering, death, and resurrection for us can enable us to cope and even to live in victory when we face life's most enormous problems.

Session 4 concludes the study by examining specific strategies our Lord has given us for confronting and overcoming our worries by His grace.

May the Lord Jesus fill your hearts with His peace as you study His Word and apply it to the worrisome situations you encounter in your lives!

Worry—What Is It? 1

Setting Our Sights

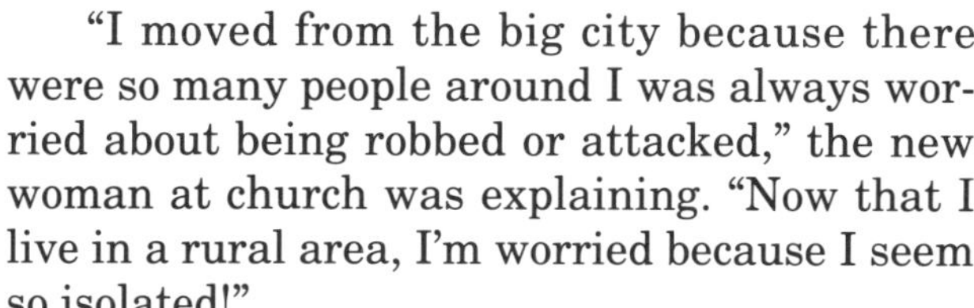

"I moved from the big city because there were so many people around I was always worried about being robbed or attacked," the new woman at church was explaining. "Now that I live in a rural area, I'm worried because I seem so isolated!"

It seems that everybody worries about something. Too many people, or too few. Am I working too hard? Am I working hard enough? Am I "balanced" in family, work, play? So many things flood in on us in everyday living. Life ratchets up our pace a notch or so every month. Or so it seems. And that doesn't count problems like our health or job security or the responsibility of aging parents or (you fill in the blank).

How do we handle so much? How do we cope with things we don't understand or don't have time to process?

Some of us (most of us?) worry. Right? But what exactly is worry, and how does it affect us? Is worry bad? We'll address these questions in this session.

Getting Started

As a group, draw a picture of a model "Worry Wart." What are his/her characteristics? How does s/he react to a worrisome situation? Keep the picture in front of you throughout this session and those that follow.

Digging In

1. How do you define worry? Write your own definition. Then have each person in the group share his/her definition. After all have shared, write a group definition of "worry."

2. Each of us experiences worry a bit differently. Each of us faces different personal challenges, and so we tend to worry about different things.

Identify some of your worries by completing the following list. Work on your own to check all the items about which you have worried at some time. You will not share specifics with anyone in your group, so be honest with yourself.

_____ Marital relationship
_____ Lack of a spouse
_____ Relationship with parents
_____ Relationship with God
_____ Habitual sin
_____ Own health
_____ Speeding ticket
_____ Deadlines
_____ Job
_____ Vacation
_____ Taxes
_____ Church issues
_____ Health of family member
_____ Financial situation
_____ Children

3. After you have completed your checklist, zero in on one of the items you find most worrisome right now.

a. How do you react when you think of this issue? Take into account both your physical and emotional responses.

b. What do you want to do in response to the worry?

Take a few minutes to write a description of your reactions.

4. We've considered a definition of worry and looked at some of the things about which we may worry. What is the effect of worry in our lives? That's easy. In a word—STRESS. The stress produces physical symptoms and emotional response. Stress may even affect us socially as we pull away from people, ashamed to admit our worries or sensing that no one can help us with our problems. How many of these effects did you include when you grew your group's model "Worry Wart?"

Hitting Home

1. The physical, emotional and social effects of worry are real. What about spiritual effects? Reconsider the worries you identified in the list on page 16.

a. How do **you** respond to God when you are worried? *(Check as many as apply.)*

____ I pull back from Him.
____ I forget to include Him in my problem.
____ I run to Him for help.
____ I feel guilty about worrying and embarrassed to ask Him for help.
____ I begin to doubt His care.
____ I get angry at Him.
____ I feel closer to Him.

b. Does your view of God change? If so, How?

c. What is it that you want to say to God when you are worried?

2. Together read the section from Jesus' Sermon on the Plain.

Then Jesus said to his disciples: "Therefore I tell you, do not worry about your life, what you will eat; or about your body, what you will wear. Life is more than food, and the body more than clothes. Consider the ravens: They do not sow or reap, they have no storeroom or barn; yet God feeds them. And how much more valuable you are than birds! Who of you by worrying can add a single hour to his life? Since you cannot do this very little thing, why do you worry about the rest?

"Consider how the lilies grow. They do not labor or spin. Yet I tell you, not even Solomon in all his splendor was dressed like one of these. If that is how God clothes the grass of the field, which is here today, and tomorrow is thrown into the fire, how much more will he clothe you, O you of little faith! And do not set your heart on what you will eat or drink; do not worry about it. For the pagan world runs after all such things, and your Father knows that you need them. But seek his kingdom, and these things will be given to you as well" (Luke 12:22–31).

a. Jesus describes some worries common to all people of all time: What will I eat (if the harvest fails, if I lose my job, if the economy slides)? What will I wear (if my credit cards reach their limit, if the guy in the senior class asks me out, if I don't lose this weight, if the river floods my house again)? What reasons does Jesus give to show we should not worry about food and clothing?

b. The word *worry* appears four times in this section. Underline *worry* each time it occurs. How would Jesus define "worry"?

c. What does Jesus call those who worry?

d. So what is the cause of worry?

3. Worry may seem to be an inevitable part of our daily lives. The frustration for the Christian is that we fall into worry when we know it's not what our Lord wants for us. We don't want to be "of little faith" in our strong God! But how do we stop worrying? How do we develop the kind of faith that evicts worry from our hearts?

a. It may sound harsh, but we've already seen the truth—worry is a sin. Jesus says, don't worry. We do it anyway. As Christians, we know what to do with sin. What?

b. What does God do then? Are you sure?

c. Find Philippians 2:13 in your own Bible. If you can, underline it. Now rewrite it in your own words, words that capture the meaning of God's promise to you personally.

d. Yielding up our worry or turning the temptation to worry over to God will work, trying hard not to worry won't. Why?

4. Our comfort comes in knowing that all of our worries are best left with God. He has the power and ability to deal with all our problems—big and small. He has the vision to see the end from the beginning in any circumstance. But how can we trust this more? How can what we know in our heads and say with our mouths settle down more and more firmly in our hearts?

a. Read Philippians 4:4–9 on p. 43. What does the Holy Spirit counsel here about combatting worrisome thoughts? Underline the appropriate words. Then summarize them here.

Wrapping Up

Heavenly Father, thank You for sending Your Son, Jesus Christ, to be my Savior. You gave so much for me, and I know you will also provide everything else I need. Still, worry is very present in my life. Forgive me for worrying. Through the merits of Your Son, Jesus, who conquered worry through a perfect trust in You, remind me again in the midst of my daily challenges of Your presence and power. Use Your Word of promise to give me new strength to trust You more fully and to seek first Your kingdom. In Jesus' name I pray. Amen.

The Extra Mile

During the coming week notice what things tend to cause you anxiety. Make a mental note of your worries. Consider the following texts. Each gives us an example of someone who is worried. Where do you see yourself in these texts? What has God done to calm your worries for you?

Luke 10:38–42
Luke 12:13–21
Romans 7:14–25

What Am I Worried About? 2

Setting Our Sights

Nothing was going right for Larry. On his way out of the house, the dog had escaped. Larry had left his wife to chase Lucky through the neighborhood. Now Larry was stuck in traffic, so he'd miss his 8:15 meeting. Larry envisioned his angry boss (this was a BIG meeting) and decided not to ask for the raise today. The cost of sending the twins to college had begun to strain the family budget to the limit. "At least they didn't make it into Harvard or Stanford," Larry thought wryly.

The car in front of him swerved just in time to miss the bumper of the car ahead of it, and traffic came to a standstill yet again. Larry continued to list his problems in his mind, while downing more Pepto-Bismol.

Larry's story may not be your story, but each of us has days when worries large and small combine to overwhelm us. In this session we'll look at the specific worries that bother us most and consider the help God offers us in time of worry.

Getting Started

1. On your own complete the following sentences. You will not be asked to share your answers with anyone, so feel free to answer honestly.

a. When I'm worried I . . .

b. When I'm not worried I . . .

c. The thing(s) about which I'm most worried right now is (are) . . .

2. Choose one other person in the group, preferably someone you don't know well. Tell your partner about a worry that you don't mind having shared with the group. It could be a current concern or a childhood worry. Be as general or as specific as you want to be.

3. Use one or two words to summarize the worry you just talked about with your partner. Print it on the question mark below. Then write the worries of the other members of your group on the question mark too.

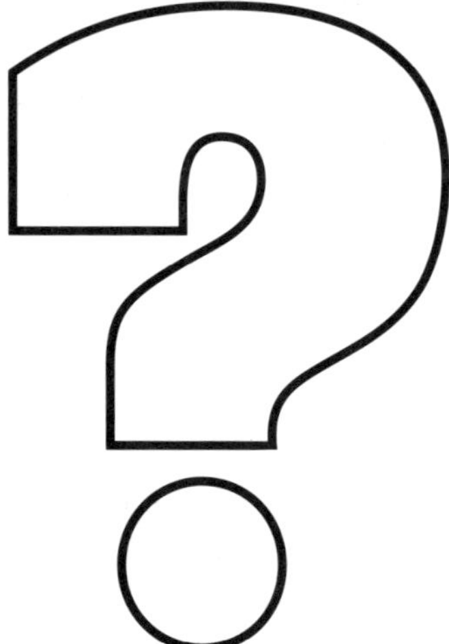

Digging In

1. Many Christians count Psalm 46 among their favorite psalms. See if, working together as a group, you can fill in the words missing from the psalm below.

❖❖❖❖❖❖❖❖❖❖❖❖❖❖❖❖❖❖❖❖❖❖❖❖❖❖❖❖❖❖

God is our refuge and ________________, an ever-present ______________________ in trouble. Therefore we will not ______________, though the earth give way and the mountains fall into the heart of the sea,

though its waters roar and foam and the mountains quake with their surging.

There is a __________________ whose streams make glad the city of God, the holy place where the Most High dwells.

God is within her, she will not fall; __________________ will help her at break of day.

Nations are in uproar, kingdoms fall; He lifts His voice, the earth melts.

The LORD ____________________ is with us; the God of Jacob is our ______________.

Come and see the works of the LORD, the desolations He has brought on the earth.

He makes wars cease to the ends of the earth; He breaks the bow and shatters the spear, He burns the shields with fire.

"Be still, and know that I am ____________; I will be exalted among the nations, I will be exalted in the earth."

The LORD Almighty is ___________ ______________________; the God of Jacob is our __________________. (Psalm 46)

❖❖❖❖❖❖❖❖❖❖❖❖❖❖❖❖❖❖❖❖❖❖❖❖❖❖❖❖❖❖

a. Go back through the psalm and circle words that describe God. Then underline phrases that describe God's works. What image of God does the psalmist paint?

b. During which specific situations in particular and, by implication, which kinds of situations in general, does the Lord promise to help His people?

c. While the psalm speaks to our individual lives, it also speaks about God's people as a group, His church. What promises does He make here concerning His church?

d. When might our Lord's promise to protect and defend His church comfort you?

2. Twice the psalmist states, "The LORD Almighty is with us; the God of Jacob is our fortress." God wants to make sure we hear that we are not alone. Think of Larry, the person you read about as this session began. Suppose you would happen to be the first person he would meet at the office when he arrives that morning. Suppose he asks to talk to you during lunch. What would you want to say to him? What do you want him to know? Talk about this with your partner. As you do so, jot some notes to yourself in the space below.

Hitting Home

1. At times we all get sucked in to thinking that we have to do everything ourselves. We talk ourselves into believing that asking for help is a sign of weakness. We may even feel guilty for not being able to "do it all." Or we may feel that if we ask for help we have somehow failed to live up to expectations—our own, those of other people, or God's.

a. In what area(s) of your life do you pride yourself for "being in control?" Jot some notes to yourself in the space below. You will not be asked to talk about this with anyone, so feel free to answer honestly.

b. What area(s) of your life seems out of control right now?Again, be honest. No one will see your response.

c. When you sense that you are not in control, upon what do you focus? Why?

2. The idea that we can control our own lives is a myth to which our culture clings with all its might. But in truth, we really control little in life. At heart, worry involves trying to take control over those things we cannot control.

a. We need God's forgiveness for the times we try to live as though we were the one in control, for the times we focus on our problems and on our own puny resources for handling those problems. Reread the last few lines of Psalm 46 ("Be still and know"). What do you think these words mean?

b. The psalms were written centuries before Christ lived on the earth. And yet Christ's manger, Christ's cross, Christ's open tomb reveal more fully than all else our Lord's glory. He was (and is) exalted among the nations and exalted in the earth. How do the manger, the cross, and the open tomb comfort you as you think about the times you try to "play God" in your life by worrying?

c. How do the manger, the cross, and the open tomb comfort you as you think about those worrisome circumstances that you cannot control?

Wrapping Up

Look back at the question mark on which you wrote the worries your group mentioned earlier. Agree to keep one another in prayer this week, especially prayer regarding the troubling circumstances each person mentioned.

Pray for each other now as you close. Choose one group member for whom you will pray. Your leader should open and close the prayer. Take turns praying one-sentence prayers for each other.

The Extra Mile

Challenge yourself to memorize Psalm 46 this week. That which we memorize stays with us; it is available so that the Holy Spirit can bring it to mind in times of celebration and of struggle. The next time you're feeling "out of control," recite the psalm to yourself. "The LORD Almighty is with us; the God of Jacob is our fortress."

A Worrier's Digest 3

Setting Our Sights

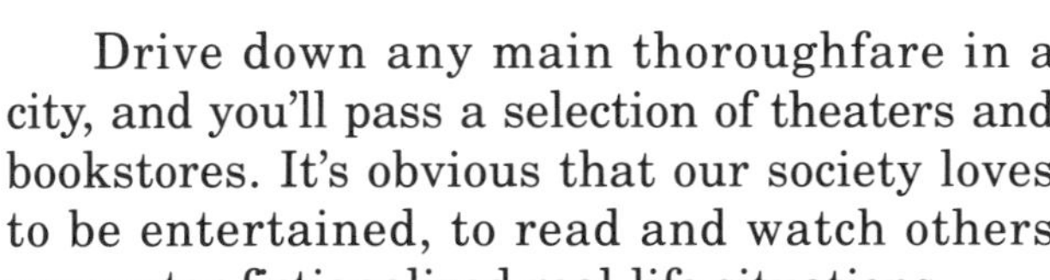

Drive down any main thoroughfare in a city, and you'll pass a selection of theaters and bookstores. It's obvious that our society loves to be entertained, to read and watch others encounter fictionalized real-life situations.

Sends your spirit soaring!
You'll leave the theater dancing.
Audiences have gone wild.
A feel-good movie.

With this kind of advertising, who wouldn't want to attend these movies? I can forget my worries for awhile and feel happier when I leave the theater.

In this session we'll encounter, not a feel-good story, but a drama born out of the trauma of real life. We'll see God's love and power active on behalf of His people during the darkest days of life. And we'll look to our heavenly Father to show Himself strong—in Jesus—on our behalf, too, even in life's most worrisome moments.

Getting Started

A number of popular, best-selling books have been made into box-office successes. These crowd-pleasers are packed with adventure, crises, drama, death, and what passes in this world for love. The good guy always wins, overcoming tremendous obsta-

cles and riding off into the sunset to live happily ever after.

If any in your group have seen recent movies like these, let them share their observations about the feel-good formula that draws people to theaters everywhere.

Digging In

The psalms are packed full of the stuff of real life—adventure, crises, drama, death, and true love. Most of them could be considered kind of mini-autobiographies, authentic records of the hurts, victories, emotions, and worship of God's Old Testament people.

1. Read one of these, Psalm 116, aloud together in your group. It's printed on p. 33.

a. In what situation did the psalmist find himself before he cried out to the Lord? List the specific problems you can identify in the space here.

b. How does the psalmist respond to what God has done for him?

I love the LORD, for He heard my voice; He heard my cry for mercy. Because He turned His ear to me, I will call on Him as long as I live.

The cords of death entangled me, the anguish of the grave came upon me; I was overcome by trouble and sorrow. Then I called on the name of the LORD "O LORD, save me!"

The LORD is gracious and righteous; our God is full of compassion. The LORD protects the simplehearted; when I was in great need, He saved me.

Be at rest once more, O my soul, for the LORD has been good to you. For You, O LORD, have delivered my soul from death, my eyes from tears, my feet from stumbling, that I may walk before the LORD in the land of the living.

I believed; therefore I said, "I am greatly afflicted." And in my dismay I said, "All men are liars."

How can I repay the LORD for all His goodness to me? I will lift up the cup of salvation and call on the name of the LORD. I will fulfill my vows to the LORD in the presence of all His people.

Precious in the sight of the LORD is the death of His saints. O LORD, truly I am Your servant; I am Your servant, the son of Your maidservant; You have freed me from my chains. I will sacrifice a thank offering to You and call on the name of the LORD. I will fulfill my vows to the LORD in the presence of all His people, in the courts of the house of the LORD—in your midst, O Jerusalem. Praise the LORD. (Psalm 116).

2. Fiction—on screen or in books—fascinates most of us. Partly because most times it is bigger than our own lives, and yet it relates to our own lives in one way or another. We usually hate, for example, to see the hero of a story die. To be sure, we want him (or her) to star in a sequel. But don't we also resist that kind of ending because deep down we squirm at the thought of our own death? If our hero dies, the movie just isn't quite as good—it comes too close to reality.

a. The writer to the Hebrews (2:15) considered the fear of death humankind's biggest worry. Why do people worry about death?

b. Go back and mark the verses in Psalm 116 that tell about the psalmist's experiences in confronting death.

c. In the space below, write a one-sentence summary of what these verses mean to you.

3. Some crises in life can be worse than death. Unemployment. Bankruptcy. The death of a loved one. Floods. Hurricanes. Tornadoes. Fires. Earthquakes. Long-term illness. Life can slam door after door in our face. We may find ourselves at the end of our strength, feeling that there's no where left to turn. That kind of powerful worry can overwhelm us. Today's psalm doesn't stop with the anguish of the psalmist facing disaster. It goes on to describe a power beyond our understanding.

a. Circle those phrases which describe this power.

b. What can this power mean for us when we face the worst life can throw at us?

c. What does this power mean for us when we face the end of our life here on earth?

Hitting Home

So many of the psalms detail the troubles of the psalmists. In this sense we can view the book of Psalms as a kind of "Worrier's Digest," a compilation of just about every distress human beings face.

Psalm 102 records a prayer rung from deep affliction.

Psalm 94 asks the Lord to avenge the injustice done to the weak.

Psalm 57 was written by a fugitive, a man on the run.

Psalm 51 begs God for His forgiveness after its author, King David, committed gross and terrible sins.

We can read our own names, we can confront the essence of our own problems as we read psalms like these.

We, too, know the defeats of daily life. We, too, are often overcome with worry about how we are going to survive the next 24 hours. Life seems to be too much for us as we dwell on what we have not accomplished, what we cannot accomplish, what we will not accomplish. And, even as we worry about the day-to-day problems of life, the fact that we will someday die throws more fuel on the fire of our worries.

When we live life like that, we live in bondage.

1. Look at Psalm 116 one more time. Read the last sentence.

a. Why can the psalmist conclude with this note of praise?

b. Read 2 Corinthians 4:13–18 (p. 37). As you do that, underline the phrases that give you particular reason to hope, to trust your Savior, despite the pressures you face.

Explain one or more of these phrases to your partner.

2. When do you find it hardest to "fix your eyes on what is unseen"?

3. How might confessing the sin of "shortsightedness" and receiving God's limitless forgiveness and love now help you later on (today,

this week, whenever) as you're tempted to worry again?

With that same spirit of faith we also believe and therefore speak, because we know that the one who raised the Lord Jesus from the dead will also raise us with Jesus and present us with you in His presence. All this is for your benefit, so that the grace that is reaching more and more people may cause thanksgiving to overflow to the glory of God.

Therefore we do not lose heart. Though outwardly we are wasting away, yet inwardly we are being renewed day by day. For our light and momentary troubles are achieving for us an eternal glory that far outweighs them all. So we fix our eyes not on what is seen, but on what is unseen. For what is seen is temporary, but what is unseen is eternal. (2 Corinthians 4:13b–18).

Wrapping Up

Work with your partner to write an unrhymed poem—a psalm of your own, if you will—about the distress you face in this present day. Use Psalm 116 as a model. Note that it delineates the psalmist's worries, but then it moves the reader to the sure and certain hope in our Lord even in the very center of life's storms.

As you pray together to close today, take turns reading what you have written, each pair of partners reading their psalm in unison until all have been read.

The Extra Mile

Each day this week, read a different psalm during your devotional time. Consider the different kinds of psalms and see if you can identify several that fit specific needs in your life (e.g., times of thanksgiving, distress, loneliness, worship, transition).

How Can I Handle My Worries? 4

Setting Our Sights

Amy got home very late. By time she finished dinner and got upstairs to the bedroom, Philip was already in bed, reading.

"What a terrible day," Amy began as she sat down at her make-up mirror and began to daub her face with cold cream.

"I don't know what we're going to do about filling that assistant manager's position. Carl had been with the firm so long. And the plumber called to tell me he can't get here until next week. And I checked my calendar—it looks like there's no way I can take my vacation on the dates you suggested. To top it all off, we got our tests back tonight in my statistics class. I think I'm flunking. I'm so tired. I just don't seem to be sleeping well right now."

Philip didn't answer. Amy turned to look. Philip, she discovered, was having no problem sleeping.

All of us at one time or another find ourselves wanting to unload our worries and frustrations. But others can't—or at least, don't—always listen. As we conclude this study on worry, we will consider ways to handle worrisome situations in ways that lead to trust in God rather than to doubt and mistrust.

Getting Started

Find a partner. Spend a few minutes sharing your answers to the two questions below and listening to your partner's responses, too.

1. To whom do you turn first when you want to talk through a problematic situation?

2. What is it about this person that draws you to him/her?

Digging In

According to legend, children in Guatemala used "worry dolls" each night. A child would tell one of the tiny dolls a worry and then place the doll under his/her pillow. If the child had multiple concerns, multiple dolls went under the pillow. In the morning, the dolls had taken away the child's worries.

1. Read Philippians 4:4–9 (p. 43). Then work through these questions with your partner.

a. What specific things does the apostle Paul direct His readers to do with their worries? Underline these commands. You should find at least six of them.

b. What two specific promises does the passage make to God's people concerning the worries they handle in the way God directs?

c. If you occupied your mind with true, noble, right, pure, lovely, admirable things,

would it be easy (or even possible) to worry? If you occupied your mind with worries, would it be easy (or even possible) to concentrate on true, noble, right, pure, lovely, admirable things? What do you think Paul is suggesting in these verses?

2. God does not leave us to face our problems alone. He promises to stay right beside us as our refuge, strength, and fortress. We read about that in Psalm 46 (session 2). He also tells us that we need to become part of a Christian community, a local congregation. God encourages us in our struggles and holds us accountable for our growth in grace through our brothers and sisters in our congregation.

a. Think about the challenges you face right now. How have your Christian brothers and sisters been there for you in that challenge?

b. What else, specifically, would you like them to do for you? Could you ask for that help? Explain.

c. What needs for help and for encouragement do you know about in the lives of your Christian brothers and sisters right now?

d. How might God want to use *you* to provide that help or word of encouragement?

e. This course is about to end. With whom in your group can you follow-up after today? Whom could you encourage? To whom could you be accountable in your struggle with worry?

Rejoice in the Lord always. I will say it again: Rejoice! Let your gentleness be evident to all. The Lord is near.

Do not be anxious about anything, but in everything, by prayer and petition, with thanksgiving, present your requests to God.

And the peace of God, which transcends all understanding, will guard your hearts and your minds in Christ Jesus.

Finally, brothers, whatever is true, whatever is noble, whatever is right, whatever is pure, whatever is lovely, whatever is admirable—if anything is excellent or praiseworthy—think about such things.

Whatever you have learned or received or heard from me, or seen in me—put it into practice. And the God of peace will be with you. (Philippians 4:4–9)

Hitting Home

In the time we have spent together in this course, we have seen our Lord inviting us to come to Him in all times of need and trouble. We have seen His promise to hear and to help us. We have seen that God wants us to focus our attention on His gracious presence and on His promises rather than on spending time thinking up ways to control uncontrollable circumstances.

We have also reminded ourselves that even though God has seen us through trials in the past and even though He promises to do so in the future, we still often fail to trust Him. We find ourselves locked in an internal civil war—the war between saint and sinner that our brother, the apostle Paul, wrote about in Romans 7.

Keep these thoughts in mind as you read Lamentations 3:21–26 on p. 45.

1. Which words from these verses assure you that God forgives sins of worry? Underline them.

2. Which words from these verses would comfort you during situations in life in which you cannot control your circumstances? Write them here.

3. Which words from the verses indicate that the writer used the same antitidote for worry St. Paul would offer centuries later?

4. If you can do so comfortably, share with your group a key insight from God's Word that you want to take away with you from the time you've spent together in these four sessions.

Yet this I call to mind and therefore I have hope: Because of the LORD's great love we are not consumed, for His compassions never fail. They are new every morning; great is Your faithfulness.

I say to myself, "The LORD is my portion; therefore I will wait for Him." The LORD is good to those whose hope is in Him, to the one who seeks Him; it is good to wait quietly for the salvation of the LORD. (Lamentations 3:21–26)

Wrapping Up

Pray together with your partner before you leave today. Ask that person what specific things to include in that prayer. Then keep that person's concerns in your prayers during the next few weeks and check back with him/her in a week or two to see how things are going.

The Extra Mile

As you get ready for bed each night for the next few days, consciously take your worries and place them in God's hands. As you turn off the light, remember that even as you sleep, your loving Savior is at work on those problems that concern you. Pray a prayer of thanks for His strong and loving attention to your individual circumstances.

Helps for the Leader

1—Worry—What Is It?

❖ Getting Started

(*About 10 minutes.*) Before you ask the group to open their books, ask several volunteers to talk about why they want to study this topic. What questions do they bring with them? What issues do they hope to address?

Then ask everyone to open their study guides and read today's goal statement ("Setting Our Sights"). If your group is new to the Connections series, you may want to skim "How to Use This Course" also. Pay particular attention to the agreement found on page 3 of this guide. Stress especially the statements about confidentiality, the "pass" option, and the importance of everyone's participation.

Then ask someone to serve as the group's "artist." Together, the group will create a picture of a "Worry Wart." Use a large piece of newsprint and colored marking pens for the portrait, if possible. Follow the directions in the study guide as you work together on the drawing. Note that you will refer to the picture throughout the course, so make sure that it will be available next time.

Note: If newsprint is unavailable, have a large piece of paper tablecloth or several sheets of typing paper taped together for your drawing.

❖ Digging In

1. (*About 5 minutes.*) Be aware that since this is your first session together, some participants may not feel comfortable sharing freely in a group. Give individuals a few moments to write their own definitions and then allow volunteers to share their thoughts. Don't force anyone to share.

Then read a definition from a good dictionary. Let the group compare their definition with the dictionary definition.

2. (*About 2 minutes.*) Read the directions to the group. Before participants begin the exercise, assure them that no one will be asked to share the specifics of their answers.

3. (*About 5 minutes.*) Again, let individuals work on this exercise. Assure them they can keep the details private.

Then discuss the exercise as a group. How many participants did not check a single item in number 2? How many checked 1–5 items? Who checked more than 5?

What kind of reactions do group members experience when they worry? Does worry attack everyone in the same way or are there differences? Talk about these questions together, but be aware of your time constraints. Move the conversation ahead as necessary to make sure you have enough time to work through the biblical material of the lesson thoroughly.

4. (*About 1 minute.*) Return briefly to the "Worry Wart." Would anyone like to add anything? Change anything? Accept reasonable responses.

❖ Hitting Home

1. (*About 5 minutes.*) Read the introductory paragraph to the group. Then give individuals time to answer questions *a–c* on their own. Again, assure them that no one will see their answers. After a few moments, ask for comments. What does worry do to our relationship with God?

2. (*About 2 minutes.*) Read the passage from Luke 12 together aloud.

a. (*About 1 minute.*) Read the paragraph to the group. Then ask them to find the appropriate words from Luke 12: "Life is more than food" ; "God feeds [the ravens]"; "how much more valuable you are"; and so on.

b. (*About 2 minutes.*) Let the group wrestle with how

Jesus might define worry. Accept responses that reflect the text you just read.

c. (*About 1 minute.*) Jesus calls those who worry (all of us), "You of little faith." The cause of worry is a lack of trust in God's care and love.

3. (*About 5 minutes.*) The first paragraph ends with two rhetorical questions. After you have read them, simply move into the exercise that follows. It outlines the process the Bible calls "repentance."

a. Perhaps no more appropriate answer can be given than to quote the apostle John, "If we confess our sins, [God] is faithful and just and will forgive us our sin and purify us from all unrighteousness" (1 John 1:9).

b. See the verse quoted above. We can be sure of our complete forgiveness because God has promised to forgive us for Jesus' sake.

c. Help participants personalize this verse as they paraphrase it. It promises that God not only gives us the power we need to *do* His will, He also supplies all we need to *want* to do His will. All we must do is receive these things from Him, open our arms and our hearts to receive them.

4. (*About 4 minutes.*) After you have read this paragraph, ask participants to turn to Phil. 4:6–9, either in their own Bibles or on p. 43. You will return to this text in session 4, so you need not deal with it fully now. Do, however, invite participants to underline as indicated and share their insights with the group. Accept reasonable answers that come from this text.

❖ Wrapping Up

(*About 1 minute.*) Pray the prayer together, perhaps holding hands around the circle in your group.

❖ The Extra Mile

Before you dismiss the group, call attention to this section of the lesson. Encourage each individual to work through these Bible passages during the coming days. Ask them to see

what insights they gain as the Holy Spirit speaks His Word to their hearts. Send the study guides home with the participants to make this study possible.

In addition, ask everyone to jot down the worries that come to mind during the days ahead. This will help them prepare for the next session.

2—What Am I Worried About?

❖ Getting Started

(*2 minutes*.) Welcome everyone warmly. Thank them for returning. Help everyone find a partner, and make sure everyone has a pen or pencil. In a prominent place, post the "Worry Wart" picture you made last time.

Ask a volunteer to read the goal statement for this session ("Setting Our Sights"). Then move into the exercises that follow.

1. (*About 3 minutes.*) Invite participants to work on this on their own. Assure them they will not be asked to share their responses. Encourage them to be honest with themselves and with our Lord.

2. (*About 3–5 minutes.*) If time and your circumstances will allow, read the poem "Whatif" by Shel Silverstein to the group. (From *A Light in the Attic*. It describes childhood fears, large and small.)

Then have group members talk with their partners as directed. Remind everyone of the "pass" option you discussed last time. Also encourage everyone to pick a worry they won't mind the whole group knowing about.

3. (*About 2 minutes.*) Each participant should summarize his/her partner's worry in one or two words while everyone prints the worries around the question mark on p. 24 in their guides. After everyone has shared, ask if all the common worries of adults have been mentioned. If not, write the additional ones the group suggests near question mark, too.

Digging In

1. (*About 3 minutes.*) Give individuals time to work at filling in the blanks of the psalm. Then read it in unison. Check a Bible for the correct wording (NIV).

a. (*About 3 minutes.*) Let participants work on their own to do this. When everyone has finished, or nearly so, read the last question ("What image of God does the psalm paint?") and ask for a response. If participants focus on God's omnipotence, majesty, and so on, keep pressing the group until someone points out that God uses all these attributes *for us*. He's strong—on our behalf. He brings peace—to us. And so on.

b. (*About 2 minutes.*) The psalm speaks specifically about terrible natural disasters and about wars. By implication, it speaks about any trouble or turmoil we may encounter.

c. (*About 2 minutes.*) Call attention to the paragraphs that begin "There is a river" and "God is within her" (verses 4–7). Let volunteers suggest words from the psalm. One main promise comes in the words *She will not fall.* Our Lord will preserve His church, regardless of how bleak that possibility may seem sometimes.

d. (*About 3 minutes.*) Invite participants to talk about this with their partners. Then ask for comments from the whole group.

2. (*About 5 minutes.*) Give participants time to jot some notes on their own. Then ask them to share with a partner. Point out that before launching into a "mini-sermon" in witnessing to someone, we do well to listen for awhile. Where does the other person really hurt? How can we best pinpoint our comments about God's Law and God's grace toward us in Jesus? Is Larry arrogant, overwhelmed, or simply at a loss for a way to live life confident in God's forgiveness and hope? Until we know the answers to those questions, we will not know whether to apply Law or Gospel to Larry in this situation.

Hitting Home

1. (*About 8 minutes.*) Have a volunteer read the opening paragraph to introduce this exercise. Then say something like, "We encourage our children to grow up into independent adults who can handle the difficult situations of life. We think of people who single-handedly overcome trauma as heroes. Movies glamorize the strong, rugged individual, the one who can take care of himself or herself. The message we send and receive in all this is that we *need* to be in control. When a situation gets to be too much for us, it often fills our thoughts. We worry about how we will survive the circumstances." Then move the group into the questions that follow.

a. Let participants answer this for themselves. Assure them no one will be asked to share their answers.

b. Again, give participants a few moments to answer.

c. Ask the group's opinion. Often we focus on ourselves or on our problem. What's significant is that we do *not* focus on our Lord and His deep love for us.

2. (*About 5 minutes.*) Read the opening paragraph. Ask whether participants agree or disagree with the statement that our culture clings to the myth that human beings can control their own lives. Ask those who volunteer an opinion to share the evidence on which they base their opinion.

a. Some versions translate "Be still" as "Cease striving" In everyday language, "Stop spinning your wheels. Relax in Me, remembering that I'm God and you're not."

Use this question to help group members review the truth that we cannot go through this world alone. We cannot live a truly independent life. Thank God we don't have to. We need not rely on ourselves for the strength we need to meet life's challenges. We have a Savior who is truly our "ever-present help" in every time of trouble. Confident in His forgiveness—yes, even for the sins of worry—we can face each new day.

b. This question gives participants the opportunity to review what God's forgiveness in the cross of Jesus Christ means as they realize their own lack of trust. It's an "old, old story," but one that all God's people love to hear (and need to hear) repeatedly.

c. Some participants may find Rom. 8:28 helpful as they think through this question. Ask each person to share thoughts with a partner.

❖ Wrapping Up

(*About 5 minutes.*) Read these suggestions to the group and urge participants to follow them. Give them time to do so.

❖ The Extra Mile

As time permits, let group members share ways they have used to memorize Scripture successfully. Encourage them to take up the challenge in the study material.

3—A Worrier's Digest

Getting Started

(*About 7 minutes.*) As in previous sessions, ask a volunteer to read the goal statement for this session ("Setting Our Sights"). Then move into the discussion in "Getting Started." Move through it quickly, avoiding getting bogged down in too much detail.

Digging In

Read the introductory paragraph to the group.

1. (*About 6 minutes.*) Follow the directions given in the study material. Then move into the questions that follow.

a. Accept reasonable responses drawn from the psalm itself.

b. Again, accept reasonable responses drawn from the psalm. Ask volunteers to read specific words of praise.

2. (*About 5 minutes.*) Ask someone to read Hebrews 2:5 from his/her own Bible to the group.

a. Let volunteers speculate.

b. Give individuals time to underline phrases on their own. Then ask for comments from the group. Accept reasonable responses. Most participants will probably cite verses 3 and 4: *The cords of death entangled me, the anguish of the grave came upon me; I was overcome by trouble and sorrow. Then I called on the name of the LORD: "O LORD, save me!"*

Others may suggest verses 8–9: *You, O LORD, have delivered my soul from death, my eyes from tears, my feet from*

stumbling, that I may walk before the Lord in the land of the living.

c. Allow individuals time to think and write. Then ask volunteers to share with the group. If members have a hard time responding, share your own response. The psalmist may have had a close encounter with death. We may not have shared that kind of experience. But most believers can think of other examples of "deliverance," instances in which our Lord has been active in our lives in obvious and powerful ways.

If no one mentions it, point out that all of us have known what it is to be overcome by the "trouble and sorrow" of sin. At the cross, Jesus conquered sin's power for us. And we have received the results of that victory each time we have called on His name to ask for forgiveness and cleansing from our sins.

3. (*About 5 minutes.*) Read the opening paragraph. Ask if participants agree or disagree. Have those who respond explain their opinion.

a. We may consider death, something over which very few of us indeed exercise control, to be humanity's biggest worry. Yet often the catastrophes mentioned in this paragraph can overwhelm us with just as potent a force. Still, in the center of the storm's fury, we can have peace. Let participants share the phrases they circled.

b. Again, let participants volunteer their thoughts. The verse you looked at as session 3 ended, Romans 8:28, has much to say about this. If time will permit, have someone read this verse. In fact, you may want to read verse 28 through the end of the chapter.

c. Psalm 116 talks about a power able to save the psalmist from death. At the same time, it describes God's heart in the words, "Precious in the sight of the Lord is the death of His saints." Our Lord wants us home with Him. Nothing, not even death, not even Satan, not even all hell's demons will keep Him from making sure His children arrive home safely when our lives here end.

❖ Hitting Home

(*About 3 minutes.*) Read the description of Psalms as a kind of "Worrier's Digest." Do the participants agree with this characterization? If not, why not? If so, what other examples can they cite to show the psalms as a compendium of human need and fear on the one hand and God's complete faithfulness on the other? In other words, which psalms would help the "Worry Wart" the group created in session 1 as he encounters the circumstances he is tempted to worry about?

1. (*About 5 minutes.*) Have a volunteer read the last sentence of Psalm 116 aloud.

a. The psalmist knows, accepts, and trusts God's ever-present help in life and in death.

b. Give individuals time to read 2 Corinthians 4:13–18 and to underline the phrases as suggested. When all have done so, ask that each person explain the phrases they've underlined to one or two people sitting near them in the group.

2. (*About 5 minutes.*) Ask volunteers to respond. You may want to begin by sharing an experience or two of your own in which you found it difficult to "fix your eyes on what is unseen."

3. (*About 2 minutes.*) This question will stimulate participants to recall the principles of 1 John 1:8–9 and Phil. 2:13—the dynamic of repentance. We live continually remembering our Baptism simply by confessing our sins, clinging to God's promise to forgive us, and yielding our lives up to God by looking to Him to provide the power to obey Him (and even the power to *want* to obey Him). We will never overcome worry, especially not the fear and worry we feel when we confront life's tragedies, by trying hard to trust God. Rather, we rely on Him to create new and trusting hearts within us (Ps. 51:10).

❖ Wrapping Up

(*About 10 minutes.*) Read the directions to the group and invite them to find one or two other people with whom they would like to work on this project. If some prefer to work alone, let them do this. Note that the poem they create will be incorporated into today's closing prayer.

Acknowledge that a believer could spend a long time crafting a "masterpiece" that, like a psalm, includes words of praise to God. Remind them that time is brief, and encourage them to pace their writing.

You might also note that the form Psalm 116 uses could be a useful guideline as they work. It begins by listing the writer's concerns and concludes with a statement of God's care and the psalmist's thanksgiving for that care.

When the group is ready, form a circle. Ask for special prayer requests. Offer those petitions first. Then organize the group so everyone knows who will read their praise poem when.

When all the poems have been read, conclude the prayer yourself by praying the last line of Psalm 116: *Praise the Lord*!

The Extra Mile

Encourage group members to use the Psalms as part of their daily devotions in the days ahead. In addition, they may choose to keep a journal, identifying psalms which they find especially meaningful for various needs or times of celebration.

4—How Can I Handle My Worries?

Getting Started

(*About 5 minutes.*) As in previous sessions, read this session's goal statement to the group ("Setting Our Sights"). Have your class "Worry Wart" posted in a prominent place. Ask each group member to find a partner and direct partners to spend a minute or two sharing their answers to the questions in "Getting Started" and a few more minutes listening to their partner's responses.

Digging In

(*About 1 minute.*) Have a volunteer read the paragraphs that describe the tradition of the worry dolls practiced by the children in Guatemala.

1. (*About 8 minutes.*) Ask a second volunteer to read Phil. 4:4–9 aloud. The group should then spend time working through the questions with their partners.

a. Individuals should underline the following phrases:

- Rejoice in the Lord always.
- Let your gentleness be evident to all.
- Do not be anxious about anything.
- In everything, by prayer and petition, with thanksgiving, present your requests to God.
- Whatever is true, whatever is noble, whatever is right, whatever is pure, whatever is lovely, whatever is admirable—if anything is excellent or praiseworthy—think about such things.

- Whatever you have learned or received or heard from me, or seen in me—put it into practice.

b. The two (or arguably three) promises are as follows:

- The Lord is near.
- The peace of God, which transcends all understanding, will guard your hearts and your minds in Christ Jesus.
- The God of peace will be with you.

You might point out that the word translated "guard" in this verse has also been translated "garrison." It is a military term that refers to heavily armed soldiers standing watch. The point Paul makes here is that our Lord wants to protect us from the damage worry can cause in our lives; He Himself has promised to stand guard over our hearts as we make use of His means of grace to renew our minds by meditating on that which is true, noble, right, and the rest.

c. The human mind generally will focus on only one thing at a time. When we occupy our minds with true, noble, right, pure, lovely, admirable things, those thoughts generally crowd out worry. Paul uses this fact to make a practical suggestion for handling our worries. Once we've done all we can do, we turn our thoughts to God's goodness and in doing so, crowd out the opportunities Satan would exploit to tempt us to worry. Ask how doing this might help your class "Worry Wart."

2. (*About 10 minutes.*) Read the opening paragraph here to the group. Then ask that individuals answer these questions on their own, jotting their thoughts down with an eye toward sharing those thoughts in a few minutes. After eveyone seems to have completed the exercise, ask that they talk with their partners about their answers, perhaps reserving the right to keep one or more answers (e.g., *e*) to themselves.

❖ Hitting Home

Read these paragraphs to the group. Then ask a volunteer to read Lam. 3:21–26.

1. (*About 1 minute.*) Give group members a moment to do this. Most will probably underline, "Because of the LORD'S great love we are not consumed, for His compassions never fail. They are new every morning; great is Your faithfulness."

2. (*About 2 minutes.*) Answer will vary. Ask volunteers to share the words they choose.

3. (*About 2 minutes.*) *I say to myself, "The LORD is my portion; therefore I will wait for Him."* Point out that the writer of Lamentations speaks God's Word to himself in times of trouble and worry. In doing so, he focuses on the most true, noble, right, pure, lovely, admirable, excellent and praiseworthy things of all.

4. (*About 5 minutes.*) Ask volunteers to answer the question for the entire group.

❖ Wrapping Up

(*About 8–10 minutes.*) Allow a few minutes of extra prayer time today. Ask that each person talk and then pray with his/her partner as directed.

❖ The Extra Mile

Encourage participants to read and practice the suggestions given here.